SCOTT MANLEY HADLEY

The Pleasure of Regret:
A Memoir of Class, Ambition & Education

BROKEN SLEEP BOOKS

Published 2020,
Broken Sleep Books:
Cornwall / Wales

brokensleepbooks.com

First Edition

Lay out your unrest.

Publisher/Editor: Aaron Kent
Editor: Charlie Baylis

Typeset in UK by Aaron Kent

Broken Sleep Books is committed to
a sustainable future for our planet,
and therefore uses print on
demand publication.

brokensleepbooks@gmail.com

ISBN: 978-1-913642-21-1

Contents

'Give us the pleasure of regret;
Our tears sound wiser
Than our laughter'

-from 'We Will Be Conscious of Our Sanctity'
by Dylan Thomas, Welsh Poet

'we're all in the gutter; but
some of us are look-
ing at the gutter'

- from 'technically-haikus.doc'
by Scott Manley Hadley, Bald Poet

the pleasure of regret

Scott Manley Hadley

'cigars', a poem in lieu of an introduction

On the final day of school
A friend's dad
Decided to give us advice.

He shared his cigars -
things he smoked but didn't enjoy –
And told us how to be men.

Mostly his words were materialism
Of the smalltown
Middle England
Conservatism
You'd expect,
But one thing he said
Stuck with me
As a fear.

My friend's father
Said to us
As if imparting an essential truth:
The problem with ageing
Is that though you'll fancy older women
You'll never stop finding young girls attractive.

Maybe he said "young girls"
Maybe he said "young women"
I do not know

If I have made him sound
More or less
Paedophilic.

I don't think his point was
That he wanted to fuck children
But he **was** kinda saying
He wanted to fuck some of our friends.

And
Really
He was saying
We shouldn't feel bad
When we – like him –
Find ourselves approaching sixty and
Still get the horn
For teens.

But I **have** felt bad
As a result of nearly all the desire I've felt
Even without
Having any desires
Society would chastise me for.

I do not think
Pre-emptive forgiveness
For inter-generational lust
Would have helped.

I think this man
Was not a man

Used to ignoring himself
And here
He confused
Arrogance
With wisdom.

We nodded and coughed out his Cubans,
Boys being schooled
On the real world.

There is
Famously
A love that dare not speak its name
But there are a thousand lusts that shout
And scream
When instead they should be
Silent.

like a pansexual roger moore

For my secondary education, I attended a grammar school.

A grammar school is a state (i.e. not private) school that students have to pass a test to attend.

Grammar schools were introduced to the UK with the idea that they would improve social mobility, but they didn't. By the time I began high school they had been phased out in the majority of the country.

I was one of the poorest students in all my classes.

For the last two years of high school, my grammar school became open to anyone who wanted to sit A levels, the exams you need to pass to attend university. My school year was about to be expanded by hundreds and hundreds of strangers: those who'd failed the grammar school entry exam and those who hadn't taken it.

There would be fresh blood.

I spent the summer imagining the friends I'd make.

I wanted leather jackets, cigarettes and hip-flasks;

I wanted indie rock and promiscuity;

I wanted eyes-open cosmopolitans;

I wanted lesbians and gays, poets and artists;

I wanted gorgeous, unattainable studs with the street smarts of the rougher school down the road and a fuck-it attitude to life;

I wanted

cool.

I wanted someone who talked about Flaubert, fellatio and fucking awesome parties.

I wanted an idol.

I wanted a hero.

I wanted a muse.

I wanted – and I got – Frank DuBois.

Frank DuBois arrived with a bang.

Frank brought hipflasks of his dad's whiskey into school.

Frank was a pack-a-day smoker and had been since he was fourteen.

Frank was tall and thin and **hairy**.

Frank had chest hair, aged sixteen!

Frank had a beard!

Frank had been the go-to-booze-buyer in his social circles since he was **thirteen**, puberty having hit him hard, fast and young.

Frank wanted liquor, Frank wanted women, Frank wanted luxury and Frank wanted adoration.

Frank wanted to project the image that I had hoped to find.

We were a perfect match.

Before we spoke, I thought Frank was aloof.

Frank was cast as the lead in the school play, which I'd fucking wanted. Once I got to know him, though, I understood.

He is – and always will be – a leading man.

He is – and was – charismatic.

At least, he is when he tries…

Frank is intelligent, and the teachers noticed.

Frank was forgiven the hangovers and the odour of cigarettes because when he bothered to contribute in class (be that by handing in an essay on time or just answering a question) he did so with near-perfection.

Frank was charming.

Frank charmed everyone, everyone liked Frank, except (perhaps) the people who saw his charm as **dangerous**. Maybe they were just the people

He never chose to direct it at.

After the school play, we went for a curry.

The curryhouse was bring your own booze, so we brought our own booze.

My friend David was very drunk and Frank invited him and I, plus a girl called Holly, back to his house. None of us had been there before, but we recognised it, because Frank lived in **the mansion with the treehouse**.

Frank's house had a huge garden, and in one corner – visible from the top deck of the bus to the next town – was a MASSIVE treehouse with a zip-wire.

Frank lived in a huge converted farmhouse with a tasteful conservatory sticking out of one side. There were four bedrooms, I think, maybe five, maybe even six. Four or five bathrooms, the main one with underfloor heating, whose warm tiles I would both pass out and ejaculate on over the following year. There was a dining room, two living rooms, a massive kitchen, a utility room, a pond and a garage with an attic.

They had everything I could imagine anyone rich owning: a study, multiple computers, multiple cars, iPod docks in every room, video games, a huge basement filled with wine and guitars, so many guitars, so many beautiful guitars, all of which Frank eventually sold.

Frank's house was envied by even the most middle class of my grammar school peers: they would stare at it through the steamed-up windows of the school bus twice a day.

This house was like a palace, and all of a sudden **I was there**, supporting the tipsy David and trying to not tell Frank and his parents, who appeared as we entered the house, how much their home had been idolised by us grammar school kids.

It was like something out of a **catalogue**.

My parents' house has always been a mess. My mother is a hoarder. The cupboard under the stairs contains every shoe owned by any of the four of us (I have a younger sister) while living in that house.

All the tiny shoes I wore as a toddler are there. As are all the cheap coats.

Throughout the house, the wallpaper is filthy.

There are records that are never played. There are ornaments that are ugly, box after box of broken pens, dry felt tips, blunt colouring pencils and melted wax crayons…

There are piles of paperwork, stacks of bills and bank statements stretching back about thirty years, if not longer.

It's a mess.

There is **crap** everywhere.

My parents' house looked "lived in", but lived in by people with no care for aesthetics. Their clothes have always been horrible, their house was too.

I walked into Frank's parents' house in the middle of the night, and found myself, for the first time, amongst designer furniture, deep, thick carpets, wine cellars, cigar collections, treehouses, a rabbit hutch the size of my sister's bedroom, a pond bigger than my parents' lounge…

This was **life**, I thought. This was what houses were **meant** to be. Artfully arranged piles of archaic farming and sporting equipment, that underfloor heating (an invention I hadn't even known existed), and in the kitchen an AGA.

An AGA, an AGA, an AGA.

Years later, I walked past the AGA factory in Ironbridge with a friend from University and I stopped and I stared and

I thought about all the time I'd spent in Frank's kitchen, all the clothes I'd watched him dry on it, all the meals I'd watched him cook, there, on the AGA. His AGA. AGAs will always make me think of that year, will always make me think of Frank.

I cried, a little, at the factory.

I'm a sentimental

Middle English

Poorly-adjusted

Man.

Frank had first had sex when he was fifteen.

He tried to keep this secret because he was ashamed of how unattractive the girl had been. She was perfectly pleasant, friendly, nice, not stupid, but she had a large, prominent birthmark on her face.

There were often rumours about this tryst, but Frank denied them for a long time because she didn't look **anything** like the women he openly dated. It was only years later that he confirmed it had happened, and by that point neither the lie nor its absence mattered.

On that first night, we were taken to the conservatory. David was put to bed, and Holly went to sleep after maybe an hour or so, too.

I worry that in my memory of this first night I combine memories from subsequent weeks, months. I don't think I do. I think this all happened together.

Frank and I sat, alone, in his conservatory, him on a large leather sofa atop a floor tiled in murky brown.

There was plate glass on three sides, and lots of plants and ornaments. A bust of something, someone, I forget who, if I ever knew. Some wellies, maybe, a coffee table, filled with *Good Housekeeping* and other glossy magazines, like *Yacht Owner* or something similar (I don't think Frank's dad had a yacht then, but he wanted one).

There was an ashtray on the table, lit candles, no, that's wrong, there were never ashtrays when Frank's parents were home, except the time his dad gave us cigars. It all merges, all the nights merge into one eternal, year-long binge. Which it basically was.

That first night, I sat on one of the metal chairs that faced the sofa. There were two of them, probably intended as garden furniture, chairs that belonged outside. There was also a wicker chair. Maybe I sat in that. Maybe I sprawled on the fluffy white rug. On later occasions I remember me and others spilling red wine on that rug and cleaning it up with salt and unoaked chardonnay.

We sat in the conservatory, late at night. Peaceful, Frank's parents also in bed. Frank slotted his iPod into the Bose dock on top of a corner cabinet and started playing *I'm Wide Awake It's Morning*. I'd never heard it before.

Now, this album always makes me weep.

That evening was when I was invited across the threshold of the upper-middle classes.

I sunk my teeth in and sucked dry every neck presented to me for as long as I could, until the point, a decade later, when my invitation would be rescinded and I'd crash back outside bloated, sick, shaking from caffeine, unable to shit solids, bursting with sexual frustration, craving cocaine and alcohol at eleven fucking forty five am and living entirely vicariously through books and television.

I sucked in everything the upper middle classes offered me, but the one thing they never offered was any fucking money.

I ended my time among the rich poorer than I began it. But that isn't Frank's fault.

I sat in a chair in this beautiful upper-middle class home, and Frank and I listened to Bright Eyes. It was his favourite album, he told me. He told me he'd given it to every lover he'd ever had.

Frank told me stories about love affairs, about three-way relationships, about partying, about staying in hotels with women… About falling in and out of love, of women who fell in and out of love with him… Of intrigue between friends, of stealing lovers and lovers being stolen back… Of broken promises and broken hearts and and and-

This was not the life that any of us had been living at the grammar school.

Frank had **lived**. Frank had been to **gigs**, Frank had been to **London**, Frank had stayed in **hotels**, Frank had stayed in **hotels with women, like James fucking Bond**.

Later I realised that most of these stories must have been – at best – exaggeration: there simply hadn't been enough **time** for everything Frank spoke about to have happened.

Frank was sixteen – even if he'd started **incredibly young**, he couldn't have had more than **three years** of bedhopping and illicit hotel trips and sleazing and philandering and behaving like Casanova.

Frank spoke to me as a seasoned and well-versed Don Juan. He spoke to me as someone who **knew the ways of women**, someone who was approaching sex from a connoisseurly perspective: no longer a base urge, something more akin to an Artist's appreciation of Art.

Frank had given *I'm Wide Awake It's Morning* to, I think, only one girl, and I don't think he ever had sex with her.

How much of my early idolisation of Frank came from him

deliberately lying, and how much from my naivety regarding the way people live?

He's been shagging for five years, a decade, longer, I thought. I believed **everything** he said. This man, this cool stud, **wanted me in his house**, wanted me **in his confidence**, wanted me to drink his bloody Jack Daniels, wanted me to know about good music and good times. He wanted to share things with me and he wanted to impress me. No one had ever tried to impress me before. I liked the attention, and Frank liked the adoration.

Frank wanted to be looked up to, and I wanted someone to look up at.

I wanted a friend who made me feel **cool**, I wanted someone progressive and modern and interesting and charming and **fun**. I wanted to be educated, and Frank wanted a pupil. He knew about many things, and I was hungry to learn.

I'd spent years as the class nerd. That was changing.

I already had a girlfriend, I'd recently started wearing contact lenses and I'd had my huge hair cut down to a more manageable – and flattering – length. I was at my teenage prime, ready to meet and mingle and **grow**.

Frank told me about love.

During the course of that 45 minute and 41 second folk album, he taught me all about his life and the aches and pains of being an aging lothario. Frank DuBois – to naïve Scott Manley Hadley – had eyes a thousand years old and a dick that was hard more often than The Times cryptic crossword.

Frank DuBois was a king, he was **the** King, he was Jagger, he was Bowie, he was Bob Dylan, he was Dylan Thomas, he was Pete Doherty, Russell Brand, Tom Jones, he was all the fucking others, all rolled into one. He was a rock star and he fucking knew it. He strutted around school with a confidence that I **knew** he deserved.

My first memory of Frank DuBois is him reclining in a chair, a rosary hanging from his open shirt, his long thin legs and his beautiful pristine boots laid on a table in front of him. He had an immaculate side parting, and managed to look both posed **and** relaxed. He was inviting looks, he was talking with animation but **poise**. He was loud but terse. Someone saw me looking at him across the classroom and whispered,

"You know the new girl with the birthmark on her face?"

"I think so."

"Frank had sex with her."

"That Frank?" I nodded in surprise towards this – to my mind – vision of mid-noughties cool, with whom I wouldn't exchange a word for weeks.

"Yeah."

That first night (or pretty soon after) I asked him about her.

"No," he said, "Of course **I** didn't sleep with **her**."

The Frank I was being introduced to, the character he was playing, was a playboy cad who made love to beautiful women in beautiful places after beautiful, thoughtful, seductions. He wasn't someone who casually fucked a woman **just because he could**.

He lied to me, to build the myth.

I don't remember when he later told me the truth, but it was during a period when we were less close.

Lying was Frank's way of making it clear he cared. If he was lying, if he was myth-building, he was **thinking about what I thought about him** and thus **thinking about me**.

The truth, he told me, when he told me, was that he was at a party, a sleepover, with a lot of girls. He often got invited to sleepovers because the girls at his school thought he was gay.

It turned out that all the bed-sharing and bed-hopping he'd mentioned before was as a platonic friend. One evening, probably drunk, everyone else went to bed and he had sex with the girl with the birthmark, in the dark, on a living room floor. He didn't enjoy it much, he said, but it made him feel more confidant and **more of a man** than before.

Every weekend, Frank and the group of hangers-on who surrounded him would meet in his conservatory and we'd drink Lambrini and Jack Daniels and Stella Artois and any wine Frank could steal from his father.

We started calling our parties bacchanals. Probably someone in the group had misread Donna Tartt.

We began to spend hours in overly-alcoholised jam sessions using the numerous guitars Frank had lying around. 'The House of the Rising Sun' and Iggy Pop's 'The Passenger' became our anthems. We improvised poetry, we skat-battled, we guitar solo-ed and harmonica solo-ed and bongo solo-ed and tambourine solo-ed until these two simple chord progressions slid deep into my heart. Now, whenever I hear either song, I smile with a melancholy nostalgia. These were the freest days of my life.

Once a girl Frank was infatuated with tried to kiss me. I rejected her because I had a girlfriend and a naïve morality, but Frank sent me home immediately just in case I wavered.

Months later, they nearly had sex, but didn't because they had no condoms. Frank shook me awake and asked me if I had any in my bag and I lied and said I didn't. This was before we kissed, but already I was possessive. I didn't want Frank fucking someone who wasn't me, even though I was fucking someone who wasn't him.

When Frank's parents were away we used to run around the garden naked. Nudity and poetry and music and liquor. Cigarettes and dinner jackets and-

I miss it.

I miss it most because I know it, and nothing like it, can never happen again. I spent ten minutes in Frank's house during the days before Christmas 2012, and it was painful.

It was, once, the house where the best moments of my adolescence occurred and, then, it was just *Frank's parents' place.*

It was where I became who I wanted to be, for a bit, there in Frank's Conservatory.

We felt so cool. We felt so young. We felt so fucking good-looking.

We could be fit and intellectual and charming and loud and naked and wasted without anything bad happening, aside from mild alcohol poisoning.

It was everything I wanted. It was everything I'd **ever** wanted, for a bit. I didn't feel like an outsider at Frank's parties. I felt like I **belonged**. I never felt that way again. No one else ever made me feel part of a group like Frank DuBois did. This is why I had to love him.

Nothing like that time could happen again. No one I like wants to live in the countryside, no one wants to form a commune and go do naked nature worship among fields and flowers. We could manufacture it for a night, a weekend, a week, maybe. But it wouldn't be the same. It felt magical because it felt like it would never end. It felt magical because I thought life would keep getting better.

It didn't.

Frank had a car, a black convertible mini.

He used to drive us around with the top down, sunglasses on, scarves flapping from our necks as we joked about Leonora Carrington and the Warwickshire countryside burned past. We used to blast music, racing between small towns like we were middle English James fucking Deans.

Shortly after Frank's 17th birthday, but before he could drive the car, my first girlfriend broke up with me.

The night we'd finally had sex, my parents were [uncharacteristically] away and I hosted a party. I lost my virginity at an event where most people were downstairs playing the military strategy board game Risk.

Like all first experiences of sex, it was mediocre.

I'm not certain if all my dick went in, and I think she made me withdraw before I came, even though I was wearing a condom.

If I was having sex with men, I remember thinking, there wouldn't be any fears about pregnancy.

We stopped having sex after a couple of months and soon after that she ended things. She was right to do so, I preferred spending time with Frank.

The only time I remember enjoying sex with her was in her bedroom on the one occasion we were **ever** alone in her house, before she and I went and babysat a child for a few hours.

I took her from behind, at her insistence, which I had thought would render sex pointless, because it was all about how **special** and **unique** the person you were with was, right, why would you make love with someone whose face you couldn't see? Sex was about romance and love, yeah, I thought: I was idealistic.

She was right, though, I did like it. I came too soon, I usually come sooner than I'd like to, but nowhere near as soon as I did when I was seventeen and having sex with a woman I wanted.

By this point I had started masturbating[1]. Once I'd received my first blow job, while watching *Ferris Bueller's Day Off*, I'd decided I could no longer deny that I wanted to.

I used to masturbate by tying the cord from my pyjamas around my cock, beneath the head, and fucking the knot. I'd ejaculate very quickly then, too. Every time I came there would be a **lot** of semen.

Nowadays, wanking takes **ages**, and very little comes out, and it usually oozes rather than explodes. I should probably go to a doctor, but I don't care as I can't see myself ever trying to conceive.

---

1   I didn't masturbate until I was 17.

Before I was 14 or 15 I'd never washed underneath my foreskin, because it hurt too much to try.

The skin I could expose smelled bad, and I could see something solid and dirty underneath.

When I finally bit my lips in agony and pulled back the bright red skin in the shower, I found a mass of yellowish, grey, coagulated mush that smelled like rank cheese.

I had to scrape it out with a fingernail. It was the texture of feta: it crumbled, it was soft.

This was the residual build-up of years of nocturnal emissions: I'd never ejaculated intentionally.

Even in my pubescent wet dreams I wouldn't reach orgasm in a blissful sexual setting, instead I would run away from the potential of sex and, in the dream, urinate. When pissing in the dream, I'd ejaculate in real life, then wake up ashamed ashamed ashamed.

The first time I retracted my foreskin it stung so much I didn't clean there again for months, and the filth built up again: quicker, this time, as I and my repressed libido were growing.

I started noticing the hidden substance crumbling off in my pants, and I knew I would have to learn to stretch myself so I could keep my penis painlessly clean.

One night during the last year of school, we got a slightly older friend to drive us into Birmingham to go to a massive indie disco. I remember making out with a woman in the Digbeth nightclub who had the biggest tongue I have ever encountered before or since and, as she ground her body against me, I ejaculated, hugely, into my pants. I cleaned myself up in the toilets and went and found Frank. I didn't tell him about what happened, though in the car back home I could smell my own cum through my trousers.

I did not feel like much of a man.

A problem I had until I was 19: I would get an erection **whenever** a girl put her tongue in my mouth.

I was regularly kissing before I was regularly masturbating, so my body was forever in a state of confused, repressed, lust.

Kissing Frank didn't make me hard, which I think (perversely) is why I enjoyed it so much.

A few weeks after my first girlfriend broke up with me, I spent hours making out with Frank in a garden at a house party. I never had another girlfriend at school: I was written off as gay, because no one believed in bisexuality back then.

I didn't have sex again for two years.

I had opportunities but I turned them down, because I was scared of coming too soon and being ridiculed or dumped or publicly shamed. But also because I wanted **LOVE**.

I started University and spent a lot of time kissing women I didn't feel comfortable having sex with and kissing men who didn't turn me on. An older woman pursued me and I let her have me. She was disappointed by the sex, but I knew I'd only improve with practice. Frank was far away.

Later that first undergraduate summer, I began a bad romance with a woman richer than Frank, more invested in self-mythologising than Frank, more self-destructive than Frank and **considerably** less interested in my happiness than Frank.

The night I met her I was with Frank in Edinburgh in the Summer of 2008, and I'd already been making out - on the other side of the same grimy underground nightclub - with a different stranger who was buying me drinks.

I was on gin and tonics, she was on MDMA. I was at my most beautiful, suggestible and naïve and I had a vaguely Frank-shaped hole in my romantic heart.

This relationship would last for almost a decade but it began to fall apart when I wanted a career. It truly fell apart when I lost my hair.

When I had a breakdown, right at the end of that later relationship, my friend who lived closest to me, the same friend who walked with me in Ironbridge, took me to hospital. Hours later, Frank came and found me because he knew something was wrong. I think he was on cocaine.

I have always wanted Frank's approval.

He is the brother, the father, the husband, I never had.

I desperately hoped to feel desire for Frank, but I didn't. I felt there was something wrong with me because I wanted to be around Frank and I wanted to hold Frank and I liked kissing Frank and I felt wild jealousy when Frank fucked other people, and whoever Frank's lovers were I always felt they weren't good enough for him, but I didn't want to have sex with Frank DuBois and these feelings felt incompatible.

I was in love with Frank, but it wasn't a sexual love.

And this wasn't me being confused due to youthful repression: I knew what desire felt like because I'd had sex and enjoyed it and I knew I wanted to have sex again, but I also knew that what I felt for Frank wasn't the same as what I'd felt for the woman in the Digbeth nightclub or what I'd felt for my first girlfriend when we were in her bedroom or what I felt when I tightened the cord from my pyjamas late at night.

I didn't know it was possible to want someone in your life forever without wanting to marry them.

Physical affection and tactility weren't things I'd known before Frank.

Friendship isn't something literature had taught me about, and everything I know, I learned from books.

I don't think Frank was ever in love with me, and I didn't realise I had been in love with him until I wasn't any more, and I didn't realise that meaningful friendships have a place and a purpose until I saw him in that Whitechapel hospital in the Summer of 2017.

Frank has always loved me. He has always interacted with me as if I existed.

There aren't many people

I can say that about.

When I lacked romance in my life, which I lacked for most of my twenties, I kept returning to thoughts of mine and Frank's garbled, teenage, confusing, love.

I've tried writing about Frank a hundred times. I was only able to do it, now, because my future is no longer a hole.

I can reminisce about that very good year because, finally, it's not the only good year that I've had.[2]

I can think about being in love with Frank without it making me upset, because if we'd had a rushed sexual romance a decade ago, we probably wouldn't still be talking now.

Frank is one of the great loves of my life.

It doesn't matter that we'll never fuck.

---

2   See: https://triumphofthenow.com/2018/12/31/scott-manley-hadleys-more-triumphant-2018/

I wrote a poem to Frank that I've been too scared to show him.

I'm scared because, even though I still use this stupid Tennessee Williams-adjacent pseudonym, it's probably more honest than everything I've written above.

Frank DuBois,
For years of my life,
I was in love with you.

If you'd asked me
I would have denied it
And if I'd asked myself
I would have denied it, too.

I wanted to love you
I think
But I didn't know
If it was something I *could* want
Should want
Did want.

The disastrous relationship
Of my twenties
Was a silver-coated lead medal.

Because
She wasn't *you*, Frank,
She wasn't *good*
like you are good.

But
She was *bad*
like you are bad.

Once
You told me
I was the only man you'd ever kissed
Who
You hadn't fucked.

Years have passed.
This is probably no longer true.
Maybe it never was.

I had kissed
Many men
When you said that
And now you have, too.

Maybe during all that time I wasted
Trying to love somebody I hated
The hate should have been self-directed.

I spent nine years
Putting all my time and emotion
Into a lover
A partner
A friend
Who simply **wasn't you**.

Of course
I was going to end up depressed.

it's so funny in a rich [wo]man's world

note: this chapter is developed from notes scrawled in late 2016

I am not real.

I do not feel real. I have not felt real for a long time.

I have not felt alive for years, but even when I felt alive I didn't feel real.

My partner and her brothers inherited a huge amount of money.

Too much money.

So much money that none of them and none of their partners or children will ever have to work.

Not so much money that it couldn't be added to, not so much money that we could eat at the finest restaurants every day forever, not so much money that we don't have friends (not friends, people we know) who have as much disposable income as we do (though acquired by work), but so much money that – unless we want to become city-hopping gourmands who live in hotels – we never have to work.

There's enough money for holidays, enough money for bills, designer clothes, meals out a couple of times a week…

There's enough money for fine wines and cocktails and cocaine and downers…

There's enough money for three day benders and two day hangovers, there's enough money to spend it running a loss-making company as a hobby…

There's enough money to stay in bed until noon most days and have screaming arguments, drunk on gin, most nights of the week, and enough money to have a misbehaved pedigree dog.

There's enough money to shop at Waitrose and have a classic car and cover regular speeding and parking fines.

There's enough money to never have to think about money.

There's enough money to not *have* to be real, to not *have* to worry about the same concerns as everyone else, to afford the finest food and booze and ignore the fear of mortality, to go on a spontaneous holiday when contemplating suicide, to share wealth and drugs and luxury with other people...

There's enough money that it doesn't matter that we're depressed, because we can buy hardback novels and top shelf gin and tickets to every show or film or gig or exhibition we might ever want to see...

There's enough money that we can sign up to every streaming service on the internet, buy video games, arrange a party, call a dealer, buy a bottle and distract ourselves whenever we need to...

There's enough money that visitors don't comment on the antidepressants and painkillers gauchely strewn about the house...

There's enough money that we can wank in the afternoon, we can try and create, we can try and do anything for work or satisfaction that we want to, but there's so much money that the slightest whiff of failure sends us back to the house – rent and consequence free – where we can pretend we're not scared and not anxious and not depressed by drinking until we disappear into the blackness of memory lapses and lost consciousness...

There's enough money that we can have crippling substance abuse issues and mental health crises that are left unresolved for fucking years, because we can quit any job we ever have and just cry and self-harm on the cold kitchen floor...

There's enough money that even though the central heating is broken, we can afford to just leave the oven on for hours instead...

There's enough money that we can avoid engaging with our problems because we're able to pretend they're not there...

There's enough money that it doesn't matter that we're too fucked up to hold down a job…

There's enough money that it doesn't matter that there's no one in my life who'd say "It's good to see you sober", because everyone that knows me likes me because I'm someone to party with, even though that isn't what I want to be any more and I haven't for years…

There's enough money that we can drop out and try to "find ourselves" once every couple of years, and there's enough money that it doesn't matter that we never have…

There's enough money that we could afford to get our dog obedience training, but there's so much money that we hold people in contempt who'd waste their *salaries* on that kind of thing…

There's so much money that money is the only thing we value, luxury is the only thing we value, good food and good booze and good times are the only things we value…

There's so much money that we *have to* value money above everything else, because without the money we'd have nothing…

There's so much money that we can close our eyes to the fact that people are only friends with us so we'll give them the spoils of affluence…

There's so much money that we pretend that constant engagement with meaningless fucking media is a satisfying cultural existence…

There's so much money that people laugh at me when I tell them I'm depressed…

There's so much money that I feel I can never leave, that only an idiot would step away from the kind of wealth most people dream of, and there's so much money that I know I could never earn anything close to that amount with the fucking qualifications and skills I have…

There's so much money that I work for free, and it makes me feel devalued and it means I give up on things because I want to be able to take pride in myself and how can I do that when people tell me that I'm essentially valueless…

There's so much money that nothing difficult is worth doing, because it'll never improve our "quality of life" in any measurable way….

There's so much money that when I cry I wipe my tears with towels that cost more than my parents spend on a weekly shop…

There's so much money that nothing I do matters, nothing I do is real, nothing has consequences and society tells me the best thing for me to do is stay here, self-medicating and self-destructive, for as long as I can, because "I'll never have it so good any other way" and there's so much money that every time I consider my earning potential subtracted by my average spending I know I cannot leave…

There's so much money that you have to become a snob to have self-respect, that you have to honestly believe that the way you live is better than the lives of other people, because even though other people aren't depressed alcoholics, aren't full of hate and rage and anger and shame, that even though they exercise and are energised and make love to people they're happy to be with and happy to wake up with and are able to respect their parents and their friends and themselves, that they know they're living right, meaningful and shameless lives…

There's so much money that I'd be a fool to leave, but there's so much money that **I do not exist**, it doesn't matter what I do and nothing, nothing, nothing, makes me feel alive other than the déjà vu-like flashbacks I get in the minutes before I pass out on my fucking back, daily, so drunk and high that I feel **youthful** again, I feel hope again, I feel like things might change for the better and I might get love and a career and happiness, but then I remember that I'm bald, I have no income, I'm a depressed loner and I realise that no one interesting would find me attractive, and that the likelihood is that were I to leave I'd be just as depressed, just as alcoholic, just as unsuccessful, but **poor**. And there's so much money here, right here, that staying put, staying where things are is **sensible**, as I'm a fucking mess and whose problems were ever diminished by poverty..?

There's so much money that I cannot leave, not while I'm this fucked up, and there's so much money that there's no incentive to fix myself, no reason to, and though I want to leave and be free and poor and everything else that entails, I'll never be ready to leave because of how much money there is and because I'll never be ready, I'll never be able to leave, so I'm stuck here, rich in cash but poor in everything else…

There's too much money to leave, but so little love that I need to.

There's too much money for either of us to be happy, and there's too much money for anyone to ever take me seriously when I try to explain how shit it is.

I love my dog, but that's not enough to centre a life on.

I don't know what to do.

I'm a sprawling mass of contradictions, like most people.

I hate my life yet do nothing to change it, I tire of my friends and my lover yet they're the only people I see.

I have morally good friends, yes, but I've pushed them away by being such a waster. It's the bad friends who say "I'm so glad to see you" when I turn up, eyes black, to parties, and it's never the *good* friends who see me and say "I'm so happy to see you sober."

I just want someone to say "It's so good to see you sober", "Well done for being sober", "Let me help you to be sober." But there's no one to do this.

When I slip up and crave intoxication my partner is pleased and excited, and goads me on. When I seek someone to hold me back there is only me – I am all that exists in my life between addiction and intoxication and happiness and health, and I'm a fucking maladjusted, unemployed loser.

Everything is weighted towards the way I don't want to go, as the result of the pisspoor life decisions I've already made.

People don't live their whole lives dealing with the fallout from a misspent youth, but that's what I've already spent a **decade** doing. I fucked my university career by selecting an institution in a "fun" city rather than the best possible school I could have attended. When I moved to London, alone but optimistic, I allowed other people to push me in directions **they thought I should go in**.

I followed advice instead of instinct, and I'm approaching 30 with only a dog in my life that I love…

I'm lonely but I'm rarely alone, I'm only *not* lonely when I'm by myself. It's only when I'm **free from anyone I don't want to be around** that I'm able to fucking relax.

I only feel the grinding despair recede when I don't have to compare myself to anyone else.

I only get to feel like my life may turn out to be fine when I can ignore all the evidence that it isn't.

I can only stay sober alone.

I have blackouts from drinking several days a week.

I've had weeks where it's every day for five, six, days in a row. I want to stop drinking, I do, but every time I tell someone that they tell me I'm fine.

I don't know what I did the night before last.

I have hours and hours and hours missing from the middle of the night, just flashes, glimpses, and weird text messages that betray a slurred hand. When my sober self, I don't recognise that urge to be sociable, I don't recognise the urge that sets in as soon as I start drinking to keep going until I disappear.

I'm lying, I do.

The urge is suicidal. I wish I was dead, and I imagine that death feels very much like it feels when my consciousness is lost but my body continues to exist. There's no feeling, no sense, just bruises, strange smells lingering on me and strange looks from people I do not recognise.

I deny culpability, hide my sober self from accusations, but I struggle to sleep at night and when I'm drying myself out, boozefree (which I try and fail to do with a regularity that says more about the reality of my addiction than most other things about me – if I didn't keep *trying* to sober up, I wouldn't *need* to) – when I'm doing that, when I'm not drinking, I turn to painkillers instead. Cocodemol tablets hidden from my partner, a packet of ibuprofen necked in an afternoon… I steal the massive prescription painkillers my mother has because of her MS. That's not sobriety, is it, it's just swapping one legal high for another.

My girlfriend has formally and repeatedly said she'd break up with me if I became teetotal, because she sees intoxication as an essential staple of enjoyment.

She regularly takes drugs with her 60-something father.

I drink until my mind goes blank because I'd like my mind to go blank and I don't have the confidence in my convictions to kill myself.

I tried, kind of, twice, four years ago.

I was braver then, but neither time worked, I didn't put the effort in.

I wanted an easy suicide, but – as they say – nothing worth having is easy.

My life hasn't developed in the four years since then, other than the dog.

A dog is not a substitute for happiness, a dog is not a substitute for a child, for a lover, for health, for hope, for a future.

A dog is a fucking shit thing to like the most out of **everything** in your life.

The dog just bit me. This isn't good enough.

Once I felt free and kissed a woman in a park. Once I felt free and kissed a woman in a pub. Once I felt free and walked 500 miles and then walked 200 more across the north of Spain, appropriating a dying religion's pilgrimage in the hope that it would pull me out of depression.

For a while it did, it gave me a sense of purpose.

Every day I would wake up in the dark and dress silently, talking to no one, and I would walk, do nothing but walk just walk; walk and walk and walk until the sun was so high in the sky it burnt the backs of my hands and the top of my bald head and it dried out my body and made me feel sick.

I walked and walked with this sense of purpose, this sense that what I was doing had a point and I had to keep walking because for the first time in my adult life I **literally knew where I was going**, what was happening to me…

There was nothing that could stop it nothing nothing nothing and I didn't have to worry and I didn't have to feel stressed or anxious and if the hostel I planned to sleep in was full, I would just walk further towards my destination, ever onwards ever closer to something achievable, something that would mean I could qualify to be a priest if I ever found god[3].

---

3   The elder generations ask: "Where are the essays and poems by millennials questioning the existence of the divine?"

Scott Manley Hadley answers: "In between all the existential crises about money and love and sex and power and politics and art and friendship and family and work and aspiration and body image and exercise and death and the search for contentment and travel and regret and shame and all the other ones, who has time for existential crises about whether or not there's a god?"

If I was ever going to find god, I'd find god while doing a pilgrimage, right, but of course I didn't find him or her or it, all I found was a sober sense of purpose, even though that purpose was a meaningless caesura from my real life.

Being a pilgrim was the best month of my life, it was the only month of my life since childhood where I wasn't constantly in fear of social interactions and what people might say to me.

When I was a pilgrim, it didn't matter that I had no hope for the future, that there was a home I had to return to after Santiago that was cold and horrible and angry.

When I was a pilgrim, I had purpose.

When I was a pilgrim, I had a respite and I **always had the option to throw myself off the cathedral at the end.**

I'm only happy now when I'm dreaming, it's what I wait for every day and what I yearn for every night. I deliberately set alarms to wake myself when I expect to be in REM in the hope I'll remember the dreams and remember the way happiness feels.

I don't have to live in her house in my dreams, I don't have to stay in this unwedded marriage for money and I don't have to feel shame for knowing almost everything I spend my daylight hours doing is morally bankrupt.

I live without love, I dream of fleeting happiness because I never find happiness when I'm awake... it's not allowed, she stops me she stops me she stops me

Once I felt free and held a woman's hand in a market square at night.

Once I felt free and read and wrote and wrote and read, but she doesn't like me writing, she doesn't like me reading, she doesn't like me crying, she doesn't like me having panic attacks.

"Don't cry," she ordered, once, "My friend is coming over."

Intoxication fills the same hole as books.

I read, I read, I read, I read, I do little more than read and reading is what I want to do with my time, what I want to fill every minute with. And reading won't kill me, reading doesn't lead to further physical and psychological decline, doesn't lead to me passing out on the bathroom floor, doesn't lead to me vomiting in my sleep, doesn't lead to self-harming, doesn't lead to regret, doesn't lead to missed appointments and missed opportunities and missed alarms, doesn't lead to cyclical depression and cocaine and sex.

Reading isn't allowed because it *excludes* her, but binge drinking is encouraged, binge drinking is allowed, binge drinking is fine.

I hate myself and see no escape. I belong to her, she has bought me and I am unable to leave.

When I began learning Spanish,
She disapproved.

She said,
"I already speak Spanish."

She said,
"How is that going to help **me**?"

my favourite lines
are the lines of poems
her favourite lines
are not

reading is my favourite thing
but I live in a home
where it is
less acceptable than coke

It will never be fixed.
It is not damaged,
It is **broken**.

There have not been cuts.
There have been amputations.

I haven't had sex
Sober
For years.

it's so funny ~~in~~ [out of] a rich [wo]man's world

─────────────────────

Though we called it a home
  It never really was one.

  It was *your house*
  That
  For a bit
  You condescended to let me sleep in.

I didn't feel I could leave her until she threw me out even though I hadn't cheated on her for years (if kissing even counts as cheating (it counted when *I* did it, but didn't when *she* did)) and every time we fucked I felt overwhelmed with guilt and shame and never felt any regret about other women (though maybe I would have if I'd fucked them instead of just flirting and (so so so so rarely) kissing).

I didn't want to have sex with her I wanted to have a family with her and I know that was a red flag a red flag a red flag but I loved her even while I hated her and I definitely hated her and I definitely loved her but not in a romantic way no not for a very long time and she hated me, she hated me, I felt it all the time and she made me feel like that hatred was what I deserved.

I was in a bad relationship and I didn't leave it even though I knew I should for years and years and years and we had a terrible sex life and the business we tried to start together didn't work (or at least wasn't working when she told me to leave her house then still expected me to work for her and feed our cat which she was keeping because a cat is less portable than a dog, though tbf the dog is a wonderful dog and the cat a mediocre cat so I definitely "won" because Cubby came with me and he loves me) and she wasn't interested in the same things as me and she used to tell me I was boring (I didn't "stop being fun", I'd say, "I stopped taking cocaine, that isn't the same thing") and this all broke down years ago and I'm still writing about it, which is kinda fucking lame, isn't it?

I remember reading *Trawl* by B. S. Johnson which he wrote when newly married but is all about the negativity of previous relationships and I remember thinking it must be awful awful awful to be in a relationship with someone who still writes about their ex[es] but now that's me too, me too, me too. I don't want to think about that time, because none of the thoughts are easy.

Some consolation is that she will never read this, because she never read my work when she claimed to love me, so why would she now?

Now, I have the emotional and geographic distance to write about her and that relationship, but I don't want to write about her and that relationship, I don't want to think about her and that relationship, but it's there, it was almost a decade of my life and there were highs (most of them illegal) but there were many many many many many many lows.

It started, it continued, it ended.
The memories remain.
Not all wounds heal,
Some wounds scar.

If I'd been gay
Or just **more worldly** when we met,
It would have never gotten to the stage it did.

Once, while driving,
I put *To Pimp A Butterfly* on
and she
turned it off
because she,
"didn't want to be insulted /
just for being white".

The only rapper /
she would listen to /
was Eminem.

Once, we went to a stately home with my parents
And my father – a poor, Parkinsonian, pensioner
(My mother, in a wheelchair and ashamed) -
Said,
"Only a rockstar would live somewhere like this"
And she scoffed and – to be fair, quietly –
Laughed in my ear about the fact
That **her** family
Owned FOUR properties
Bigger than this.

This wasn't the end of that moment
Though
She would bring it up
Again and again
For years
Telling people
(Who of course didn't have multiple mansions in the
family because so few people do and she did not socialise
with people who she couldn't feel superior to)
How ignorant
Scott's
Dull-witted
Labourer
Dying
Father
Is to
The opulence
Scott spends his miserable time within.

My mother went to one of their houses:
The hilltop hamlet
Converted into a **luxury mansion** (not a tautology)
In the countryside outside Siena.

It is one of the most beautiful places I've ever been
And my mother was simultaneously overwhelmed
and bored.

But my father's comment meant
My mother had never *explained* that Tuscan trip
To him
Because if she had
He would have understood
The affluence I was close to.

Every time the millionaire brought it up
And laughed again
Into an uncomfortable silence
It reminded me of the paucity of connection
Between my parents.

I am poorer than them, now,
And on a different continent,
But it is the lack of communication between them
That keeps me from resenting the distance.

My parents are contemptible
Not because they are uneducated and sick
But because they didn't believe themselves
Deserving of happiness:

i.e.

Deserving of a partner

They could actually talk to.

I am not actively pursuing my own happiness.

I am

Getting sadder.

But I'd rather be dead by my own hand at forty

Than, like my mother, dying alongside someone I don't

talk to

Who is nightly

Pissing

My bed.

her uncle
a horror writer
who read
some of my work
once said
and he meant it kindly

"your boyfriend has"
he said

"an intriguing outsider voice.
it's probably"
he said
"because
he didn't go to Oxbridge"[4]

---

4   I did get an interview
at Oxford.

I did get that far.

I fucked it
Because I had no idea how
To behave
In that situation.

They put you up
In a student room
When they interview you
And it was the first time
I'd had a room to myself

In a place

That wasn't my parents'.

I remember buying

An EP by Babyshambles from an Oxford HMV

I remember seeing a poster advertising

Hannibal Rising

In an Oxford Waterstones

I remember flirting with a woman

With a very big jaw

Who invited me back to her room

Presumably for sex

But I (as I would to so many offers of sex over the coming years)

turned her down.

In the musty office

Where I had the interview

I remember trying to talk about Oscar Wilde

Oscar Wilde

Oscar Wilde

Oscar Wilde

And trying not to talk about

The Dan Brown novel I'd been reading

On the train south.

Dorian Grey

Never lost his hair

Dorian Grey

Didn't botch

His university interview

Thinking

Instead

About terrible popular culture.

They fuck you up, your rich older lovers.
They fucking mean to, and they do.

my mother, from a distance

note: first drafted in Spring 2014 as part of a 'Life Writing' course led by Blake Morrison

My father has Parkinson's disease[5] and my mother, too, has a long-term health problem. And with hers there is concrete evidence that it's genetic, hereditary, thus likely to afflict me too. It was not discovered until about eighteen months ago.

My mother has MS, Multiple Sclerosis. She struggles to stand up for long periods of time, she has little energy, she sometimes walks as slowly as my father shuffles, she is prone to overwrought, public explosions of emotion and she now has slight-to-severe difficulty in every aspect of her life.

MS is unpredictable. It is difficult, almost impossible, to guarantee the symptoms and effects. It is a condition made crueller by the inclusion of surprise.

Sometimes when I see my mother, she is fine: happy and working hard. She has been for walks in the countryside, she has gone to nearby theatres or cinemas, she has applied for a new course, she has had a breakthrough with one of the children she works with, she has stayed up until midnight every day for a month writing essays, planning lessons, making resources and finding new ways and new things to learn. There are still days when she is able to stroll for miles beside the rivers and canals that criss-cross the part of

---

5   See my essay *My Father, From A Distance*, available as a chapbook (with illustrations by Kofi Boamah) from Selcouth Station Press or online, in a less-developed form, at https://www.berfrois. com/2018/10/scott-manley-hadley-my-father/

the country she lives in; when she can work eighteen hours without rest; when she can do new and difficult things that would have terrified her younger self.

Yet at other times she is a physical wreck in denial of her weakness.

A few weeks ago, my mother came to London for a conference. She and a colleague travelled down on a Monday evening and stayed with me overnight. I took them for a cocktail and then pizza.

My mother's colleague, Helen, who I'd never met before, had a daughter who went to school with me. This girl, one of the few – like me – from our little post-industrial Birmingham suburb rather than the leafy villages of Warwickshire, dropped out aged sixteen to have a baby.

No one saw this coming. Her name was Sarah. She was tall, quiet, had shoulder-length straight brown hair and was academically successful. She did her homework on time and was never in trouble. But, after what happened, and being from our town, she became another statistic confirming the vitriol of the posher kids. Yeah, they'd say, typical of a girl from Redditch, isn't it, getting pregnant at sixteen?

Sex was a moral failure, wasn't it?

Sex was the kind of thing the kids who smoked and might not go to university did. Not like us. *Not like Sarah.*

But Helen, more than aware that I knew that she knew that I knew her eldest daughter had dropped out of school to have a scandalbaby, didn't mention the child, who must be about ten by now.

'Who was that teacher you and Sarah had, the handsome one?' she asked over dessert, suddenly honing in on the period of her grandchild's conception.

'Which subject?'

'He used to think all his teachers were handsome,' muttered my mother.[6]

6   I vividly remember

on the cusp of puberty

'Your class teacher, he taught Economics or Business, I think?'

'Mr Young?'

'That's it. Sarah saw him recently, in Leamington. You know he's running the sixth form now?'

'I'd heard that, yeah,' I said, 'Nice man.' I realised this was the moment to ask a question. 'And Sarah, err... how's she doing?'

'She's well. Very well.'

I waited for the gossip.

'She's really well.'

Later I asked my mother, as we walked home, if I could ask Helen about her grandchild.

'No,' she told me, 'That's her business.'

---

my granddad inviting me to watch

something on the television

filled with women in bikinis

and my mother

scoffing at him

Saying

'Oh, Scott won't be interested in that'.

It was said mockingly but with resignation,

Almost as if I wouldn't understand what she meant:

My mother thought I was gay.

And even though I'd been living with a woman for years,

My mother continued to think I was gay in 2014.

My mother hangs net curtains in the windows at the front of her house. I have never known what she is trying to hide.

My nan was in hospital when she was told she had days to live. In the bed opposite her, in the terminal cancer ward of one of the shittiest hospitals in the country, was a woman of a similar age to her, part of a large Muslim family.

The woman died, as my nan lay watching, unable to move, and a stream of relatives came to see the body and they cried and screamed and wailed. My mother was affected by this, quite strongly, and spoke about it for weeks afterward, during the whole of my nan's prolonged death.

'They were so emotional,' she said, 'All of them, it must've been ten, twelve, different people who came to visit and they just screamed and cried.'

My mother didn't say this with a middle-Englander "Urgh, what a racket" tone, but with one of **awed respect**. Given the choking, self-silencing noises she made as we filed out of the crematorium a week later, my mother clearly wished she could express her emotion in a manner as vocal, theatrical and performative as those she saw opposite the bed she had sat beside.

My mother is very repressed. She won't speak about things that upset her, and this, the first death of a parent, upset her greatly. If she had expressed her grief publicly, she would've felt ashamed of herself. She wouldn't allow herself to cry how she **needed** to.

There's crying so everyone in the ward can hear, and there's crying so only your family can hear. And my mother refrained even from the latter.

My mother doesn't tell people she has MS. Though her employer and the Disability Officer of the University she attends know, it is a secret from everyone else outside of her immediate family. Other than the people I've told at parties, which is just a load of hipsters she's never going to meet.

Long ago I resigned myself to an early destructive death due to the double-generational Parkinson's of my father and his mother, so there isn't much for me to fear from another vague potential problem with my body. So I tell people. I believe fears lose potency when discussed. I'm not anxious about my inevitable destruction if I'm making jokes about it to people I barely know, right?

But my mother likes to be boxed in. She likes her problems to be hers.

When I was a teenager, my mother returned to education. She left school with basically no qualifications, and she decided to get some. A few years previously she had begun to work in a school as a teaching assistant. She was praised by her superiors, and told that if she enjoyed the work she should get a professional qualification and a specialisation, so they could justify paying her more.

She chose to work with children with special educational needs, believing that this was where she could make the most impact. Her niche selected, she began to study.

And then she discovered that she *loved* learning. In the eight or nine years since, she has climbed, part-time, higher and higher, past Foundation Degree to actual degree and is now reaching for a PGCE, her goal to become a teacher.

These essays and late nights in colleges and universities began almost thirty years after she had last written anything longer than a postcard. Yet she grew in confidence. Her grades were better than average, her tutors liked her commitment and her colleagues were impressed. She gained more important and difficult jobs, eventually being employed by the County Council to travel between schools assessing the provisions for children with special educational needs. Sadly, she was made redundant following the cuts to education made by the Coalition government.

But she kept going, she kept studying, and she kept applying the ideas she had learnt to her daily practice. Back in a school, she was taking lessons and liaising with parents and this is the stage she is at now. Perhaps less than she had hoped, but close to what she wants, close.

The majority of this has been achieved since my father's Parkinson's diagnosis. Maybe that spurred her on, but it wasn't what spurred her to *start*. The impetus was internal. She decided to change who she was and she went out and bloody did it. Right the fuck on, mother. Right the fuck on.

After the conference, I met my mother and Helen outside the venue, one of the big hotels just off Russell Square. As it was still relatively early and they had a couple of hours before their train, I suggested we visit the British Museum.

I am aware that my mother tires easily now, so I made sure to check she was OK with a five-minute walk. She said she was, and she seemed so. We walked around the square: I pointed to the first-floor room in a gorgeous townhouse (part of Birkbeck) where I'd once had Spanish lessons; I told them about the Cabmen's Shelter on the northwest corner; I gestured towards Senate House and gave the obligatory Hitler-wanted-it-for-his-headquarters factlet. We walked on.

I go to the British Museum a lot, I know it well. I took my guests through the room sponsored by the Wellcome Trust, into the glass-domed bit and over to the section full of the best things the British ever stole. My mother sat on a bench in the room with the museum's most controversial exhibits and I enjoyed looking at them in peace. The last time I was there I'd been with my girlfriend, who works in the antiques trade and has incredibly loud opinions about restitution. ('There's a bloody receipt for these marbles, and the Rosetta Stone we stole from the *French*.') But that time, in a room softly lit beneath a black skylight, I was able to contemplate in silence the timelessness of art. Even with my ailing mother close by, I could be lost in thoughts of the ancients.

When the museum closed, we left and decided to walk towards Soho. I asked my mother what she wanted to do, if she wanted to sit down, if she wanted a tea or a coffee or a cake or a cocktail or a sandwich or a wine or a g and t or a browse in a shop or anything, really, it was up to her. But she wouldn't decide.

I looked to Helen for an opinion, but she didn't offer one either. 'I'm happy to do whatever,' she said.

So, we walked through the gates and out onto the street, the metallic glare from taxicab roofs a rhythmic glimmer. It had rained, and the world had a sour, heavy, look to it, as did my mother. By the time we reached the end of the museum's railings she'd begun to stop every five or so steps to look around, using the pretence of architectural observance to disguise the fact that she was in pain.

She had told me, specifically, to not tell her colleague that she has MS. She had told me to make sure I made no allusions, accidental references or slips at any point, and I was trying my fucking hardest to not say, 'You look exhausted, let's sit down.' What I said instead was, 'Why don't we duck into this pub right here for a drink or a tea or a water? Or the café next door?'

But 'No,' she said, 'Let's keep going, I like the buildings.'

You're closing your eyes in fucking pain when you raise your head to look at them, mother. And I know for a fact that you don't give a shit about architecture because I took you – at great personal expense – to Tuscany for your fiftieth birthday a couple of years ago, and you seemed so blithely underwhelmed and underappreciative that it was weeks before I'd take your phone calls again.

'Are you sure,' I ventured, 'You don't want to grab a drink or a coffee, have a bit of a recharge?'

And again she told me she didn't want or need one, and I didn't want to tell her what to do.

I appealed to Helen. 'What about you,' I tried to joke, 'Can you make a decision?'

And she looked at me, a flutter of confusion passing over her face before she again refused to comment. She was looking at my mother as she gripped the railings of a shopfront and leant against the metal for support.

I didn't want her attention on my mother's weakness, so I tried to be distracting. I told anecdotes I'd stolen from other people, I improvised architectural analyses of the buildings my mother was resting her vision on. And eventually we moved on. But she got slower and slower.

'I think,' I said, passing another cafe, 'we should go in here.' But she *wanted* to carry on, even though she had to pause every few steps.

'Are you alright?' Helen asked, moments from breaking through the fog of illusion.

'Yes,' my mother lied, 'I'm just taking it slowly, enjoying the street. I don't see London very often. Is this too slow for you?'

'No, of course not,' Helen fiddled with something in her handbag. 'Of course not.' She avoided my mother's eye, but, like me, was too bloody English to say out loud what needed to be said.

My mother's refusals to stop walking meant that soon there then came before us a one hundred metre stretch of road, from Great Russell Street down to New Oxford Street, with nowhere offering an indoor spot to rest.

'You sure you don't want to stop?' I asked.

'Yes,' my mother lied.

And she couldn't do it, of course she couldn't do it. It took over ten minutes to cover a distance athletes can cover in ten seconds as she paused then paused then paused to pretend to study brickwork. What is the point of this, I wanted to scream.

I KNEW she was too tired to walk anywhere, SHE KNEW she was too tired to walk anywhere, HELEN KNEW she was too tired to walk anywhere. Why couldn't we talk about it?

My mother is ashamed of looking weak, but if that's her fear then she shouldn't make decisions that result in clear demonstrations of her illness. What is making her look unwell is her stubborn denial of her body's changing needs.

She'd been sent to London to attend a conference. I get it, she's more important now, she has a job where she's **listened to**.

But she's not listening to herself.

I don't worry that her physical weakness is insurmountable, I worry that her *denial* of it is.

It is only by acknowledging a problem that one can begin to address it.

Which is something she's done before. That's why it's frustrating to see her *lack* of acceptance of this new personal reality.

I can imagine what it's like.

You go years, decades, bumbling along. Your horizons are small, you're not unhappy because you never really think about unhappiness as an option. Then, all of a sudden, you decide **that's not fucking good enough**. That you are *every bit* as willing to work as other people; *every bit* as willing to try. You do something *no one in your family* but your teenage son has done before and slowly, like kicking from the bottom of a deep pool, swim towards the light of Higher Education. It shimmers there through the water, the mortarboards and the gowns of cinematic montage, the certificates on the walls of TV lawyers and doctors, the letters after the names on mastheads and credits. It is touchable, it is *there*. And you kick upwards, and as you kick you feel your legs getting tired and your chest getting heavy, but you keep going. As you kick, your knees start to ache and your breath starts to slow, and you realise your husband of thirty years won't be swimming with you, that he's content to stay on the bottom with tabloids, Five Live and an ever-more unsteady shake. But you move and it's a struggle and your father has heart problems and your mother has cancer and your daughter won't fucking work and your son is covered in bruises he pretends you're too stupid to notice, but you push, push, push and it's so difficult with no one to help, no buoyancy. Husband doesn't understand, parents conservative and ill, daughter resentful because out of nowhere there's another person in the family getting qualifications and praise from employers and all of a sudden it's not just her absent brother she's worse than, it's her *trying-really-fucking-hard* mother, too; but you, but you, but you go, you get there, you breach the surface and you smile and you get *your* mortarboard and *your* gown and *your* certificate but there's no one there to take your photograph, there's no one there to applaud and cheer for you; your husband's either working one of his last few years of unskilled labour or watching young men he doesn't know play with a ball; your daughter's probably asleep and your son's probably crying and self-medicating because he can't find the words to write "the next great novel" and that's *more important to him than you are.* You stretch your neck, you breathe the air. But the glow, that light, it's not a shining pot of gold, it's not the floodlit entrance to the graduation party of your dreams, it's not a choir of angels heralding your ascension to the intelligentsia, it's not even the laconic flash of your daughter's iPhone as she snaps a lazy pic; it's a weak flame, it's a candle, running to the end of its wick. You've done all this, late in your life, only to be told, when you go and ask a doctor if there's anything wrong with your legs after all that swimming, you've got Multiple Sclerosis, which means what? It means you could go blind, incontinent, unable to walk, speak, write, or just DIE without any warning at any point. And you'll almost certainly die before you're seventy. You taste the water and it's salt. The tears that should've been shed. But you're stoic, aren't you? You're going to keep bloody going.

But her body can't keep going like it used to, not all the time.

She had to hold my arm and lean on me for support for the last stretch of the walk, Helen nervously stepping around and asking if she's alright, only to hear words denying the visual evidence.

What did Helen think? That she was witnessing a collapse, a heart attack, someone about to drop dead? By refusing to say, 'I'm not very well and sometimes I suffer from fatigue,' my mother was forcing her concerned colleague, friend, to guess.

As we sidled into the Pret A Manger on New Oxford Street and I ran round seeking a chair, my mother braced herself against a wall and Helen tried to cheer her up by engaging her on topics she knew my mother knew how to talk about.

My mother is scared that people will judge her when they find out about her illness. She thinks that she will be treated differently, abused and bullied and mocked.

She has a Disabled Parking Badge, but refuses to use it in her hometown in case anyone she knows sees it.

My mother telling people about her MS won't make the problem go away, but it will stop *being scared of telling people about it* from becoming a problem of its own.

You rarely get help if you don't ask for it, and you never do if you don't accept it.

The coffee was mediocre, Helen provided the bulk of the conversation. Afterwards we stepped into the street and I hailed them a cab.

'It was nice to meet you,' Helen said.

'Yes, you too,' I replied, 'Tell Sarah I said hello.'

I hugged my mother, who was crying, still too tired to stand steady. She got in the car.

'Thank your girlfriend for letting us stay,' said Helen, as she awkwardly kissed me on the cheek.

'I will do.'

Close to my face she asked, 'Is your mum OK?'

I took a deep breath.

'Yeah,' I lied, 'She's fine.'

under the lectern

first drafted in the Summer of 2017 immediately after attending 'Under the Volcano, 70 Years On: A Malcolm Lowry Conference'

Malcolm Lowry (1909 – 1957) published two novels during his lifetime: *Ultramarine* (1933) and *Under The Volcano* (1947). The first was written while he was a Cambridge undergraduate and was about his gap year, which even at the time wasn't *that* original a concept. After graduating from his fancy university, Lowry went off the rails, living in Cuernavaca, Mexico, as his first marriage deteriorated, and then in a shack just outside Vancouver once he'd remarried. Lowry was an alcoholic, who'd switch from terrible binges to strict sobriety, working concurrently on multiple projects in bursts of creativity that he couldn't sustain, barely finishing any of his potential books. There was one major exception.

Under the Volcano — broadly considered (by those who've read it) a masterpiece — took Lowry almost a decade to write, rewrite, edit and complete, and he still noted potential edits years after publication. During the two and a half decades between his undergraduate novel's publication and his death by misadventure in a dull little village in Sussex, he developed a huge array of prose and poetic works, barely any of which made it into print until after his death.

The cache of Lowry's unpublished manuscripts included texts such as *Hear Us O Lord From Heaven Thy Dwelling Place* and *Lunar Caustic* (the first a collection of short stories and the second a novella), both of which were almost finished[7]. There have been the standard "dead writer" publications of poems and letters, plus two novels edited from his notes by his second wife, Margerie Bonnar, *Dark As The Grave Wherein My Friend Is Laid* (great) and *October Ferry to Gabriola* (less so). More recently, there have been academic editions published of **less** complete texts, including the novels *In Ballast To The White Sea* and *La Mordida*, as well as a bizarre "screenplay" of *Tender Is The Night* that he and his wife worked on for a very long time without having been commissioned[8]. Lowry wrote a lot but finished little, his writing deeply affecting and often beautiful, but he rarely felt confident that he had achieved with it what he wanted. Lowry wrote because he wanted to make art, but his perfectionist streak was more accurately a neurosis. He wanted to write and be read, but he did not feel himself *good enough* to deserve either.

---

7   In fact, *Lunar Caustic* was published in a French translation in 1955. Even after its French publication, though, Lowry continued to edit the text.

8   It's basically a novel-length prose description of a film (think Geoff Dyer's *Zona*) but one that doesn't exist. The imagined film combines the narrative of Fitzgerald's best novel with narratives from Lowry's own life and fiction. If it had been *deliberately* written as a piece of postmodern experimentalism it would be lauded, however as it was a self-conscious "let's make Hollywood money" scheme from people with no understanding of standard ways to format a screenplay, it has ended up merely a literary curiosity for the Lowry superfan.

Alas, Lowry died from an overdose of alcohol and prescription medication[9] a decade after the internationally-lauded *Under the Volcano* was released, having not published another book[10]. Lowry was tragic, Lowry's life was bleak. I find his texts — which are heady reflections of his life — deeply fascinating, and that is why I booked myself a place at 'Under the Volcano, 70 Years On: A Malcolm Lowry Conference' at Liverpool John Moores University at the end of July 2017. It was an academic conference (by academics, for academics), but I am not an academic. I don't quite know *what* I am, to be honest, but I thought an academic conference might distract me from my age-inappropriate ennui for a few days.

---

9   Ahead of his time!

10   Other than the French translation of *Lunar Caustic* mentioned in the footnote above.

I recently had a breakdown, and before I hit rock bottom[11] I considered applying for a PhD.

I never expected to want this, as when I completed my MA I felt committed to *never* setting foot in an educational institution again. As my life took multiple negative turns, though, I found myself looking back to the year I spent doing little more than reading and writing about books as a halcyon period, ignoring the voices in my head saying things like:

"Academia isn't real, especially postgraduate English Literature."

"Reading and writing about books isn't *engaging* with the world, is it?"

"You'd be living an idealistic life off the back of undergraduates paying sky high fees for education."

"Academics write for other academics, it's a closed circle only ever pierced by outsiders when they skimread academic texts as undergraduates to crowbar quotations into essays they've already written."

"Academics inhabit a monklike role outside of normal society."

"It would be peterpanning, wouldn't it? Which isn't good. Right? Get a job."

"Academia isn't lucrative; money — though inherently evil — has its uses, and some of those uses are fun. You enjoy travel, don't you, and (other than travelling to conferences) academics are tied to their libraries, right?"

"Academia would get boring; you like books and you like writing about books, but there's no way

---

11   See: https://triumphofthenow.com/2017/08/10/on-not-be-ing-suicidal-anymore/

you'd find the same things fascinating for the length of a career, is there? Look at your actual fucking CV."

I was desperate to escape the depressed hole I was sinking into, so defied these voices and booked my ticket to this academic conference to see how I liked dipping my fingertip in the water. By the time the conference rolled around, my mental health had caused me to lose my home, my job, my long term relationship and any belief that I could ever achieve anything. As a gift to my more-optimistic, younger, self, I still got on the train to Liverpool, even though it meant leaving my dog behind in London.

That evening, a few steps away from Liverpool's bombed-out church of Saint Luke, I sat alone in my cheap Airbnb room swiping right on every Liverpudlian woman Tinder offered me, until I reached its daily limit. I didn't get a single match, which was probably for the best. I went to bed early, mournfully masturbated and fell asleep thinking of my dog.

I arrived at the Liverpool John Moores at 9am and threw myself at the free coffee and biscuits. With my mouth full, I worried about how much I stood out, not only because of my shaved head and bright, patterned clothes (which make me stand out in most places outside of Hackney), but also because of my age. Of the 50 or so people in attendance, there were **at absolute maximum** four people there under 40, and I (then 28) was at least five years younger than all but one of those.

Lowry is clearly not attracting young academics. Or, maybe he is, but not in the UK or at any overseas universities that cover travel costs for PhD candidates studying a dead English drunk. Because — though it wasn't youthful — it was a *very* international conference. There were several speakers from both the UK and Canada (the latter home to the Lowry archive), and others from countries including New Zealand, Spain and Belgium. Lowry has inspired academics in many parts of the world, and though the speeches differed in their opinions, all shared a real interest in the work and life of this writer from the Wirral. The delegation was also much less male and pale than I had been expecting, which somehow made me feel better about myself.

The first speaker was Sherrill Grace, a Canadian academic who spoke at length about the links between Lowry and other writers, and how there is something intense and serious in his work that speaks with potency to many people.

Some of the speeches were engaging in the way I'd hoped — energetic, urgent, personal — though others veered towards the kind of off-putting *academese* I had been worried the whole conference would consist of[12]. Of the 17 or so speakers, most offered insights into readings of Lowry's texts that I had never considered. An especially engaging lecture from someone called Ben Clarke discussed the ways that class informs Lowry's portrayals of life at sea (Lowry spent his gap year as a sailor), and how Lowry's writing is more focused on the "myth" of the sea rather than its reality.

There were lectures on Lowry's interest in cinema, on his interest in the Kabbalah, on his use of ashes as a recurring motif and on the way he is "haunted" by books. A speaker called Chris Ackerley spoke about the importance and pleasures of rigorous readings, while Belgian academic Vik Doyen discussed editing the in-progress manuscripts of *October Ferry to Gabriola* in the pursuit of a version that he believes Lowry could have considered complete.

All these lectures — ranging in length from twenty minutes to about an hour — came from people who care passionately and deeply about literature and about Lowry in particular,

---

12   One speech included the phrase "place is inherently mobile", which I copied into my notes with the annotation "No it isn't". Then again, that speech went on to say that (possibly paraphrasing, my notes don't clarify) "colonialism is a history of spoilation", which is inarguably accurate.

just like me. And given the price of admission, it was *incredible* value for money: for just over £50 I received 10 hours of lectures, a live music gig, a coach tour of the Wirral (where Lowry grew up), *multiple* free tequilas and several wines and beers[13], two meals, barrel loads of tea and coffee and many, many little packets of (tbf cheap) biscuits.

How was the Malcolm Lowry Conference so cheap, I wondered? Because it's *subsidised*. As too were *all* the academics in attendance. These people only get to do this (read books, write essays, travel across the world to read the essays) because the undergraduate student fees of thousands of people — in combination with government and charitable grants — pay for their salaries. And even though I know this is "how academia works", there is something about undergraduates' fees being used to supply non-entities like myself with free tequila that makes me deeply uncomfortable.

---

13   The fact that there was free booze felt inappropriate. Lowry was an alcoholic; his life (and – lest we forget – his literary output) was ravaged by drinking. Lowry would have loved a free bar, but he also would have hated himself for succumbing to it. (I had just about enough alcohol to stop feeling too shy to social-ise, which is the same amount that means I'm too intoxicated to socialise without risk of embarrassment, so I left early, to return to another ten minutes of fruitless Tinder swiping. Boohoo.)

Although the Malcolm Lowry Conference wasn't peopled solely by heterosexual white middle-aged men, there was one demographic in which there seemed to be essentially zero variety: *class*.

Everyone present had that sense of entitlement to intellectual engagement with cultural products that is characteristic of *not being working class*. There was no mention of the mountains of student debt[14] this subsidised event relied on, or the fact that academic essays on Lowry are only read by — at best — the delegates in the room and maybe the same amount of people outside of it. The many subsidise the few: academia is a microcosm of society itself, but it is the ability to accrue knowledge for knowledge's sake – rather than money – that gets funnelled upwards. I – obviously – heard no regret from academics in their sixties and seventies about having dedicated their lives to the pursuit of knowledge in lieu, for

---

14   I began University in the last years of the New Labour government, so my debts began at "only" about £30,000. My sister, who entered higher education *after* the Lib Dems had reneged on their key manifesto pledge to not raise student tuition fees, graduated owing almost twice that. Under the system as it operated then, my sister and I were entitled to extra-large student loans due to our parents' low income, which – though *low* – was slightly *too high* for us to receive any but the tiniest of debt-free grants. These extra-large loans still presumed sizeable hand-outs from a student's parents, which wasn't an option for us. So, I worked throughout my undergraduate degree and my sister lived with our parents. As you can imagine, both of these choices impacted on the value we each took from our courses.

example, of the pursuit of *cash*. There was no *shame* from these people for having been able to dedicate their entire lives to cultural study when, in the same world, people die from a lack of food and basic medication.

The academics, the readers, the thinkers... some professional, some — like me — amateur, were all linked by class and intellectual interest. These people included the best Malcolm Lowry scholars in the world, and I was able to listen to them talk and it was amazing, even though in my head I was simultaneously worrying about money, my future, my health, my dog, my parents and everything else I usually worry about. For weeks before the conference I had been unable to read or write due to my terrible mental health, and seeing people who present themselves as if they *never stop* reading and writing, despite the continual shit the world flings towards fans, my disgust at their disconnect evaporated and rained down as something else.

I love the works of Malcolm Lowry. But I lack the talent, persistence and — let's be honest — *readership* to make writing about Lowry a viable, commercial, concern. I write about books all the time (mostly for free), and I love doing it, but I write about books when I'm not exerting my energy on things I've been culturally conditioned to value more, i.e. trying to accrue *capital*. Writing about books very rarely makes me money, yet I spend more time doing it than just about any other activity in my life. When I'm doing paid, usually menial, work I'm often distracted by thoughts of literature, but knowing that I will get to sit down with a good piece of prose or poetry is what I have always used to get through the depressing realities of my rarely-pleasant day-to-day existence.

When I look to my future, my first concern is "where will I live and how will I pay for it?"; answering this question trumps all other concerns. Successful academics haven't got to their position by worrying about cash. I *don't mean* that every academic was "born into money", but that every academic – all of whom are (in theory) intelligent and articulate individuals – has chosen to *not* use their intelligence to pursue wealth, but rather to pursue *knowledge*. You don't climb the academic ladder because you want to be *wealthy*, you get tenure (and thus some kind of security) because your work is deemed important (for whatever reason) to the department. Nobody makes great art (or anything else) while they're *distracted*: even the anxious, depressed and addicted people who make great art drift outside of their problems when they sit down to write, paint, sculpt or sing. Like Lowry, for example.

Academics are medieval monks producing texts only for a privileged few, but like monks they have a strength of purpose and a belief in the importance of their choice. **No one becomes an academic by accident** – it is competitive and bureaucratic and poorly paid (relative to other careers that demand intensive long-term study). And to my depressed, unfulfilled eyes, all the academics at the conference were happy and engaged, and even when they disagreed with each other they argued with light and fire in their eyes. These weren't people *embarrassed* by a lifetime spent inside books, they were fired up and embiggened *because* they'd spent a lifetime inside books.

I'd love to leap into academia and write on books and think about books and do nothing else, but I know I'd worry too much about inter-departmental politics, about budgeting, about staff assessments and about tawdry, bullshit little pointless things that distract and detract from potential intellectual engagement. And maybe, in reality, that **is** the life of most of these academics, but that isn't what defines them to outsiders like myself, and that isn't the side of their life that is evidenced in books and at conferences and on their CVs. Someone with an academic career may have spent a lot of time doing paperwork, marking, teaching and rewriting the same old opinion for different journals, but they are doing all of this for the opportunity to read and think and discuss and *engage*. To be engaged, to have that engagement as your identity, as your purpose: to be *allowed to* "do" reading books for a living, even if that requires administrative, external, bullshit. Imagine it: reading for a living. It sounds too good to be true. Maybe it is.

I envy these academics their determination, their focus, their refusal to give up and manage a bank or a shop or a restaurant or something.[15]

Academia may be a withdrawal from "the world of work", but it's an *enviable* withdrawal. I *wish* I felt my thinking and writing was more important than everything else in my life, but I don't. Maybe I *would* be happiest if I dropped everything and moved to Vancouver to bury myself in the Lowry archive and write a thesis that less than fifty people would ever read.

But this doesn't *feel* like something I can let myself do. I had a psychological collapse because I'm bad at listening to myself, because I internalise criticism that I need to ignore, because I pretended that my own happiness didn't need to be an active concern in my life. Why do I feel that academia is invalid when it is the mode of existence that best matches what I want from my time on earth? Or do I only want it because all I know of it is an idea, a stereotype: daydreams of leafy quadrangles somewhere with a sea breeze, mornings spent lecturing, afternoons spent writing, the evenings spent cracking open a small bottle of gin and marking undergraduate essays? It sounds like bliss, blissful unrealistic bliss...

---

15   At time of first drafting, I was managing a cinema in Brixton. At time of editing for publication, I am part of the team managing a *much bigger* cinema in Toronto.

In theory, every single academic essay seeks to do something more important than the work I do for money; every essay *should* seek to explore, expand and share *knowledge*, and it is *knowledge* that makes us more than animal, because without books, we would have no history, no science, no culture, and without these things we would be nothing but living automatons, like bees, like maggots, like ants. But are academics the only people who write books? No. And, of course, many academics churn out essays for *no purpose other than to hit publishing targets as part of their contracts*, which surely invalidates the whole justification for academia. If an academic is just another commodifiable employee who has "targets" to hit, then what the fuck is the point?

Surely surely surely every academic must have the *intention* of expanding human knowledge? Because this as a *pursuit* in itself is something valuable, far more than most of us seek to achieve when we clock in for work. When I've finished writing today, I'm going to work for just above minimum wage in a precarious job, earning *only just* enough money to cover food, dog insurance and the other few things I require to stay alive. I don't know if I want to live in a world where even the people whose work is meant to be *more* than this approach their day-to-day lives with the same attitude. If academia is a career, not a calling, then it is no better than the demeaning hospitality work I do for money, and if academia isn't a beacon of the best of our species, what is? If academia is a capitalist pursuit, then why don't we just smash the walls and gorge on cement orgies until we explode? If the pursuit of knowledge isn't sacred, then *nothing* is sacred, and if nothing is sacred, then *everything* is dust.

I know that I contribute nothing to bolster humanity with my professional time. I like to think that academics and scholars *intend* and *attempt* to do something of merit every time they sit down to think. I like to think that every time an essay is produced – even if nobody reads or learns from it – its intention was pure. But it probably wasn't. Because if there is no better life to aspire to, maybe I was right to have always been depressed. Maybe the depression and the self-hatred is a justifiable response. And that can't be true, as it's an idea rooted in the kind of opinions that only dickheads have.

I have long felt there is an alternative and elusive world of thoughtful abstraction that I can't enter because I'm trapped outside it by my anxieties about money and social interactions and health and sex and my dog and politics and terrorism and—

I thought about becoming an academic while suicidal because I thought it might hold the potential for a perfect life. I hate the "real world" and would *love* to wall myself up away from it, like in *The Bell Jar* but more successfully. I don't want to kill myself, but I don't want to live in the world in which I'm alive.

I think I would be happier if I could climb a hallowed spire and establish myself at the top with a library, but I think I'd still get distracted looking out of the windows and feeling hungry and horny and thirsty and guilty. My mind isn't **pure** enough, **focused** enough, **detached** enough, to be an academic. I'd love for my life to be centred on literature, but then I'd never eat, I'd never walk my dog and I'd never get to travel. My outsider perspective of the academic life is fantastical, I know that, but I also know that it's not something I'll ever know more intimately because I've been culturally conditioned to see it as *not for me*.

Maybe my love of literature, my pisspoor mental health, my interest in Lowry (a man from a wealthy family who lived in near-poverty) and my envy of academia all come from the same root: my class displacement felt when, most of a lifetime ago, I rocked up to a rural grammar school as the Brummie-accented child of an unskilled factory labourer. If my formative years hadn't been filled with people dismissing my *voice*, maybe I'd be an adult who trusted his own opinions more.

I'm jealous of *the idea of academics*, is what I'm trying to say. I think I'd like to be one, but I don't really know what one is and I don't want to burst the imaginative bubble by finding out.

I've been firmly made to feel that academia is not a choice for me. I've been made to feel that avarice is not a sin, that instead its *absence* is. I can't be an academic, because the only academic I'd want to be couldn't possibly exist.

I don't know what to do.

I don't know who to be.

I am sad.

I am confused.

I am..?

a timeline

1988 – Birth.

1989 – Nothing

  to   of

1999 –   interest.

2000 – My mother is a childminder and my father an unskilled factory labourer. I enrol, as one of the poorest students, at a middle class rural grammar school (selective but not fee-paying).

2001– Lots

  to   of

2003 –   bullying.

2004 – I first kiss a girl.

2005 – I begin my first relationship and start binge drinking. I meet Frank DuBois.

2006 – My first relationship ends. I notice the signs of early onset hairloss. I first kiss a boy. I stop eating meat.

2007 – I begin university. I kiss many boys and many girls.

2008 – I first visit mental health professionals. I have a fling. Later, at the Edinburgh Festival Fringe, I meet an older, affluent, woman and we begin a long-distance relationship.

2009 – My father is diagnosed with Parkinson's disease.

2010 – I finish my degree and move to London at the behest of the older, affluent, woman. I work mindless jobs for pocket money and live between her and her family's various London properties. I begin consuming large amounts of drugs and alcohol. I am semi-violently mugged, i.e. I am beaten and bruised, but suffer no [physical] injuries that don't heal within a week.

2011 – Partying and mind-numbing office work. I am predominantly intoxicated or hungover.

2012 – I start writing regularly and cut down my use of intoxicants. I am diagnosed with anxiety and depression. Around this time I begin self-harming by punching myself in the face, which continues on and off until 2017. In the background, the London Olympics. I try and fail to become a YouTube rapper.

2013 – I return to University, after my grandmother is diagnosed with terminal cancer and unexpectedly gives me enough money to pay for a Master's degree. My mother is diagnosed with Multiple Sclerosis. I spend a month backpacking in Southern Europe. I resume heavy drug and alcohol use. Two half-arsed suicide attempts. I am first prescribed SSRIs. I meet the woman I will later marry, though we are not romantically involved for many years.

2014 – I return to full time work and my health improves. My grandmother dies. I attend group therapy sessions for social anxiety. I take a second course of SSRIs.

2015 – My hairloss becomes so severe I shave my head. After I kiss another woman, my partner begins openly and constantly policing who I socialise with and monitoring where I am at all times. I receive an unexpected Christmas bonus and decide to buy a dog.

2016 – I buy a dog and name him Cubby, after Albert "Cubby" Broccoli. My partner demands I quit my job and help her run a loss-making business. I spend a month hiking alone in Spain. I begin therapy with a skilled professional and try but fail to make plans to leave the increasingly-toxic relationship.

2017 – I again resume drinking heavily (though no drugs, and the drinking is mostly alone) until I have a severe psychological collapse. A third half-arsed suicide attempt. When I am at my lowest, my partner evicts me from her house, though expects me to continue working, unpaid, for her loss-making business. I spend time quasi-homeless and end up thousands of pounds in debt due to a doomed plan to move onto a houseboat. I am prescribed a high dose of SSRIs (which I remain on to date), Valium (briefly) and be-ta-blockers. I serve a pizza to Timothy Dalton. I read my writing in front of strangers for the first time. My paternal grandfather dies. I talk about being bald on BBC3. I "date". It is a difficult year.

2018 – I fall in love and leave London[16]. *Bad Boy Poet*, my first book, is published by Open Pen. It is a good year.

2019 – Everything calms down and for the first time in years I'm able to open my old notebooks and collate this collection. My medication dose is increased.

2020 – I am diagnosed with Borderline Personality Disorder. I am prescribed anti-psychotics. I make plans to get married. There is a global pandemic. *the pleasure of regret* is published. It is sad and indiscreet, as am I, as am I, as am I.

---

16   A man who is tired of

Hearing

"A man who is tired of London, is tired of life"

Is tired of London.

afterword – borderline personality disorder

It's disconcerting, to see your life pathologised on Wikipedia.

For over a decade of my life, I've been in and out of doctors' surgeries and the stuffy offices of NHS and [low cost] private counsellors, but each time anyone gave me a diagnosis it didn't feel right.

I was told I had PTSD.

I was told I had depression.

I was told I had anxiety.

Social anxiety.

Anxiety/depression.

Anxiety/depression/PTSD.

It turns out there's a single phrase that means exactly this: borderline

personality

disorder

It sounds extreme, right?

It sounds like I have a personality that is on the borderline of being a personality.

It sounds like the description of someone who flits between personalities like schizophrenics in bad movies.

It doesn't sound like nothing.

It doesn't sound demur.

I read through the Wikipedia article on Borderline Personality Disorder the evening after I met the psychiatrist. Almost everything it said about the typical sufferer of Borderline Personality Disorder was true about me.

Have I demonstrated a pattern of idealisation and then disparagement of other people?

Yes.

Do I run away from social situations and try to avoid seeing anybody more than once?

Yes.

Have I self-harmed? Self-medicated? Done risky and dangerous things, made rash life-changing decisions or failed to make decisions that then resulted in decisions being made for me?

Yes.

Have I ever made big financial misdecisions, have I ever had persistent feelings of bleak hopelessness but also periods of hyper excitement?

Do I not know how to behave? Do I feel most comfortable around others when I'm denying and repressing my personality and my opinions and my emotions?

Am I clocked out, most of the time, from every conversation I'm a part of?

Do I regret too much?

Do I share too much?

Do I have conflicting and contradictory opinions and attitudes and behaviours?

Do I judge myself and others extremely firmly, taking dialectical, unnuanced positions?

Do I not make sense to other people?

Do I not make sense to myself?

The answer to all of these questions is yes.

I have never felt so known as when I read that Wikipedia article.

I have never felt so predictable.

I have never felt so tired of myself and so

boring

boring

fucking

dull.

"Who I am" and "what has happened to me" is a "type".

It is a "disorder".

I am officially "not normal".

The way I am is medically "wrong".

Borderline Personality Disorder is – I have newly learned – often the result of a coping mechanism gone wrong. It is what happens when people are invalidated, when the validity of their emotions and their thoughts and their experiences are denied.

It is what happens when you tell a child its sadness, its happiness, its energy, its excitement, is unwelcome and inappropriate.

It is what happens when you have a regional accent bullied out of you, it is what happens when you are mocked until you change how you appear to others, it is what happens when your achievements are derided and it is what happens when your academic decline post puberty is utterly ignored by every single person who knows you.

It is what happens when you are told you don't fuck right, when you are told you don't eat right, when you are told you don't dress right, when you are told you don't read right and when you are told you don't write right.

It is what happens when you attempt to be a different person for everyone you meet, when you try to be what you *think* the other person wants you to be and you feel like you have to you have to you have to

get it right

because

you don't want to be hit and shouted at again and you don't want to be thrown away, rejected, forgotten.

It's easier to withdraw, detach, close down, than it is to be present.

I live in a city, now, where I have no friends.

I ran away from London, like a bald Dick Whittington. I am **always** running away, like a bald dick.

I have always **wanted** to run away. I have always **needed** to.

A diagnosis and the targeted treatment that can now be given won't help immediately: one cannot erase, through a few words in a windowless doctor's office one rainy afternoon, a near-entire lifetime of trying – and failing – to be all the completely different people that I kept guessing I was trying to be.

I still don't know *who* I am, but at least I have a three word phrase to tell me *what* I am.

We are all defined by the experiences that we live through.

Sometimes those experiences

really fuck us up.

I have

A thousand regrets

But still

Even I

Take pleasure

In nostalgia

Further Reading & Acknowledgements

Use the below web addresses to access further writing by me, Scott Manley Hadley, on some of the texts mentioned above:

Dyer, Geoff, *Zona*:
https://triumphofthenow.com/2016/02/02/zona-by-geoff-dyer/

Lowry, Malcolm: *Dark As The Grave Wherein My Friend is Laid*:
https://triumphofthenow.com/2014/03/13/review-dark-as-the-grave-wherein-my-friend-is-laid-by-malcolm-lowry/

Lowry, Malcolm: *Hear Us O Lord From Heaven Thy Dwelling Place*: https://triumphofthenow.com/2013/09/16/hear-us-o-lord-from-heaven-thy-dwelling-place-by-malcolm-lowry-book-review/

Lowry, Malcolm: *In Ballast To The White Sea*: https://triumphofthenow.com/2015/02/15/review-in-ballast-to-the-white-sea-a-scholarly-edition-by-malcolm-lowry/

Lowry, Malcolm: *Lunar Caustic*:
https://triumphofthenow.com/2014/01/14/review-lunar-caustic-by-malcolm-lowry/

Lowry, Malcolm: *October Ferry to Gabriola*:
https://triumphofthenow.com/2015/05/28/review-october-ferry-to-gabriola-by-malcolm-lowry/

Lowry, Malcolm: *The Cinema of Malcolm Lowry: A Scholarly Edition of Lowry's Tender Is The Night*:
https://triumphofthenow.com/2014/11/15/review-the-cinema-of-malcolm-lowry-a-scholary-edition-of-lowrys-tender-is-the-night/

Earlier versions of 'cigars' and the poem that ends the chapter 'like a pansexual roger moore' were published in the zines *foxhole* and *rivista letteraria*. Thanks to the editors of those magazines, Dr. Jane Frances Dunlop, Fernando Sdrigotti, Ed Kiely and (for 'my mother, from a distance' only) Blake Morrison's Life Writing workshop in the Spring of 2014 for essential editorial advice.

Thanks to Cubby, my metaphorical rock (and literal dog).

LAY OUT YOUR UNREST